EVERYTHING
WILL BE OKAY!

EVERYTHING
WILL BE OKAY!

AFFIRMATIONS
& SELF-CARE
REMINDERS
FROM
YOUR PUP

HANNAH SIMPSON

weldon**owen**

INTRODUCTION

I've always had a passion for illustrating animals and have been doing so since I was able to hold a pen. When my partner and I adopted our dog, Mac, in 2021, we quickly discovered that he had an endless list of behavioral problems, and it felt like we were the only people in the world struggling to help him—even though we knew we weren't. Eventually, I decided to create an Instagram account to share our experiences working with Mac with some lighthearted illustrations in the hope of encouraging others to join our conversation. We quickly discovered that Mac's challenges were, in many ways, metaphors for dealing with the difficulties that life throws at us. My illustrations soon broadened to apply to both humans and our beloved canine friends to help people see the funny, quirkier side of everyday struggles we commonly encounter.

This book is a love letter to anyone who might need some encouragement and reassurance that they are not alone. My hope is that it will serve as a gentle reminder that you deserve to be happy, to celebrate who you are, and, like Mac, to take each day at a time and find the hidden humor in life's inevitable challenges.

Lastly, I'd like to dedicate this book to my wonderfully complex boy, Mac. This book simply wouldn't exist without you.

U. Simpson

TAKE YOUR TIME, IT ISN'T A RACE.

LOVE WHO
YOU ARE.

DON'T BE
AFRAID TO
ASK FOR HELP.

TAKE **TIME**
FOR **YOURSELF.**

IT'S OKAY
TO REST.

SLOW
PROGRESS
IS STILL
PROGRESS.

FINISH

EMBRACE UNCERTAINTY.

BAD DAYS WILL PASS.

APPRECIATE
SMALL JOYS.

FOCUS ON THE THINGS THAT BRING YOU HAPPINESS.

KEEP GROWING.

IT'S NEVER
TOO LATE TO START.

YOU
ARE
MAGICAL!

SELF-LOVE is IMPORTANT.

FIND PEACE WITHIN YOURSELF.

DON'T WORRY ABOUT THE OPINIONS OF OTHERS.

DON'T LET **ANYONE** ELSE DEFINE **YOU.**

IT'S **OKAY** TO BE **DIFFERENT**.

OUR
DIFFERENCES
MAKE US
WONDERFUL.

DON'T BE AFRAID TO BE YOURSELF.

YOU ARE PERFECT AS YOU ARE.

WE'RE ALL GOOD AT DIFFERENT THINGS.

DON'T APOLOGIZE FOR YOUR FEELINGS.

OFF DAYS ARE OKAY!

IT'S OKAY
TO BE SCARED.

SPEND MORE TIME IN NATURE.

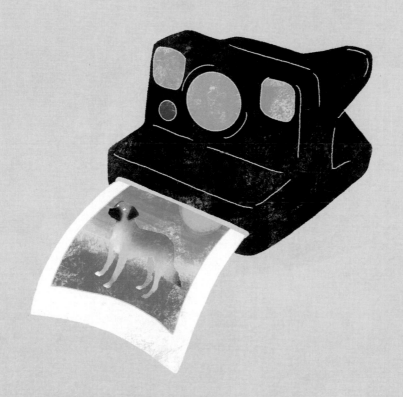

TAKE **MORE** PHOTOS.

SURROUND YOURSELF WITH THOSE WHO MAKE YOU HAPPY.

BE GENTLE WITH YOURSELF AND OTHERS.

TEND TO YOUR LIFE
WITH KINDNESS.

IT'S COOL
TO BE KIND.

CHOOSE YOURSELF.

TRUST THE UNIVERSE.

FIND **FRIENDS** IN **UNLIKELY** PLACES.

YOU ARE PREPARED FOR ANYTHING!

DON'T LET FEAR of
CHANGE STOP YOU.

IT TAKES AS LONG
AS IT TAKES.

BE YOURSELF,
UNAPOLOGETICALLY.

DON'T BE AFRAID TO LOOK SILLY.

BEING SCARED LOOKS DIFFERENT ON EVERYONE.

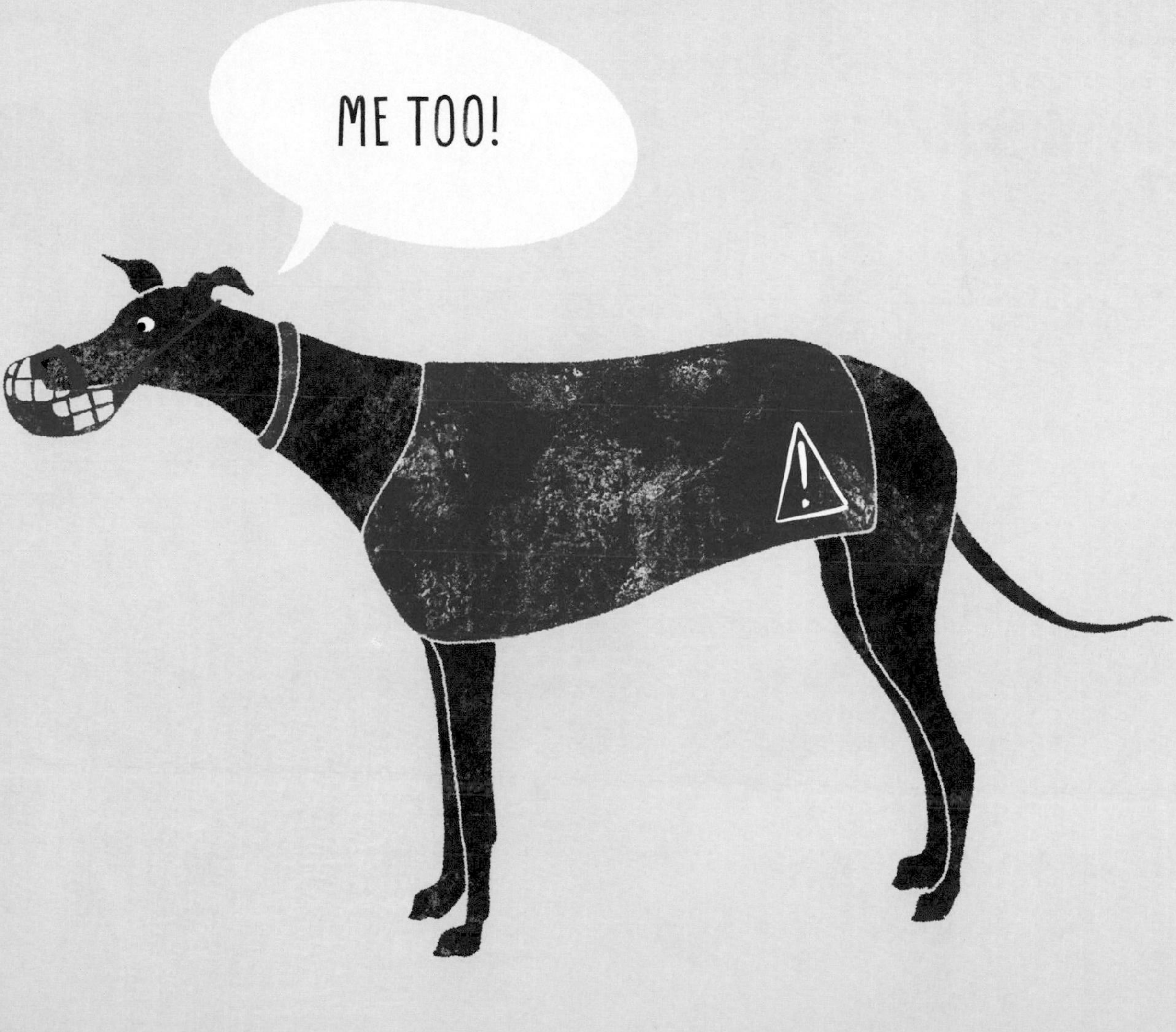
ME TOO!

BE PROUD OF WHERE YOU ARE.

YOU ARE **BRAVE** FOR **TRYING.**

YOU ARE
EXACTLY
WHERE YOU
NEED TO BE.

EVERYONE'S PROGRESS LOOKS DIFFERENT.

SOMETIMES YOU JUST HAVE TO TAKE a LEAP of FAITH.

LEAD WITH LOVE.

CELEBRATE MILESTONES, BIG AND SMALL.

YOU ARE DOING YOUR BEST.

YOU ARE
ENOUGH
AS YOU ARE.

SAYING "NO" IS OKAY!

YOU CAN **CHANGE** THE **COURSE** OF YOUR LIFE WHENEVER YOU **WANT.**

KNOW YOUR WORTH.

YOU DESERVE
GOOD THINGS.

IT'S **IMPORTANT** TO **FORGIVE** YOURSELF.

NOT BEING OKAY IS OKAY.

WE ARE ALL
A WORK IN
PROGRESS.

YOUR FEELINGS ARE VALID.

I FEEL SAD.

CHOOSE TO BE CURIOUS.

YOU ARE
NOT ALONE
IN YOUR
STRUGGLES.

YOU ARE
BRILLIANT
AS YOU ARE.

YOU ARE LOVED.

TALK TO YOURSELF
THE WAY YOU
TALK TO OTHERS.

DON'T FORGET TO

TAKE CARE

OF YOURSELF.

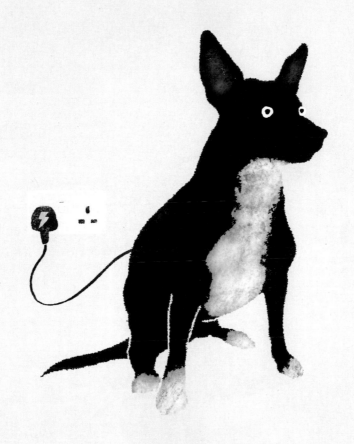

HOW YOU **RECHARGE** IS UP TO YOU.

BIG OR SMALL, YOUR FEELINGS ARE VALID.

YOU ARE STRONGER THAN YOU KNOW.

YOU DESERVE TO BE **HAPPY.**

SOMETIMES

IT'S GOOD

TO HIDE

FROM THE WORLD.

PROGRESS <u>ISN'T</u> LINEAR.

IT TAKES
COURAGE
TO BE
VULNERABLE.

BEING SOCIABLE DOESN'T DEFINE YOUR WORTH.

IT'S OKAY
IF YOU NEED
SPACE.

STAYING HOME IS OKAY.

PUT
YOURSELF
FIRST.

WEAR WHAT
MAKES YOU FEEL GOOD.

LET GO OF THINGS THAT NO LONGER SERVE YOU.

CELEBRATE

YOURSELF

FOR WHO YOU ARE.

weldon**owen**

an imprint of Insight Editions
P.O. Box 3088
San Rafael, CA 94912
www.weldonowen.com

CEO Raoul Goff
VP Publisher Roger Shaw
Editorial Director Katie Killebrew
Senior Editor John Foster
Editorial Assistant Kayla Belser
VP, Creative Director Chrissy Kwasnik
Art Director Ashley Quackenbush
Senior Designer Stephanie Odeh
VP Manufacturing Alix Nicholaeff
Sr Production Manager Joshua Smith
Sr Production Manager Subsidiary Rights Lina s Palma-Temena

Text and Illustrations © 2024 Hannah Simpson

ISBN: 979-8-88674-084-4

Manufactured in China by Insight Editions
10 9 8 7 6 5 4 3 2 1

ROOTS of PEACE
REPLANTED PAPER

Insight Editions, in association with Roots of Peace, will plant two trees for each tree used in
the manufacturing of this book. Roots of Peace is an internationally renowned humanitarian
organization dedicated to eradicating land mines worldwide and converting war-torn lands
into productive farms and wildlife habitats. Roots of Peace will plant two million fruit and
nut trees in Afghanistan and provide farmers there with the skills and support necessary for
sustainable land use.